MELT IT!

"Incredible... my favourite"

—Mike Myers

"Beyond genre"

—*Guardian*

"A legend"

—Bill Bailey

"As funny as it is painful"

—*Chortle*

"A living saint"

—Stewart Lee

"My friends are all fans"

—Phill Jupitus

"The Iceman soars and fails, but always soars again"

—*List*

"A figure of mythic proportions"

—*Independent*

"Such a riposte to showbiz"

—Neil Mullarkey

"Entirely unusual... inexplicable... don't expect anything you've ever seen before"

—*Stage*

"One of my highlights... truly a performance artist"

—Jo Brand

"Crazy stuff"

—Ruby Wax

"Brilliant"

—Simon Munnery

"No two shows are the same"

—*Independent*

"It's about time, isn't it?"

—Jools Holland

"This act is shit!"

—Chris Tarrant

"Coventry"

—Spike Milligan

This edition first published 2022

Go Faster Stripe Ltd.
21 Hanover Street, Canton, Cardiff, CF5 1LS
www.gofasterstripe.com

Cover and typesetting by Ryan Vance
Artwork photography and RFH photography by Finn Bush
Polaroid photography and cover art by the Iceman and aim
"Iceman in the Wilderness" painting by Gerald Woolley
A CIP record for this book is available from the British Library

ISBN 978-1-8384571-5-0
Catalogue number GFS-137

Printed in Great Britain by POD Worldwide

MELT IT!

THE BOOK OF THE ICEMAN

ANTHONY IRVINE & ROBERT WRINGHAM

To
Antarctica

CONTENTS

FOREWORD

Back in the day (late 80's-early 90's), it was the cabaret circuit we were on, not the comedy circuit it became. There were comedians but there were also singers, poets, jugglers, magicians, and other acts not easily categorised, but perhaps best bracketed under performance art. Chris Lynam, Andrew Bailey, Martin Soan to name but three.

And the Iceman. He used to melt ice. That was his act. I remember watching him at the Rub-a-Dub club in Sydenham, the back room of a pub called the Greyhound.

As I recall, he came on stage and *instead of talking through the microphone* he methodically set up a rickety structure, perhaps partially made of bamboo, on which he placed a large block of ice.

This was block number one hundred and twenty-five. He then proceeded to melt the ice, using various methods—friction, a hair dryer, a blow torch perhaps, with varying degrees of success—but as he pointed out "it will melt anyway".

I was in stitches. I got a pint in the bar next door, finding it hilarious *even though I wasn't in the room watching*. I still find it hilarious, in retrospect, all these years later. "This isn't an act, I'm doing it for real" he said. Absurd beautiful art.

SIMON MUNNERY
BEDFORD
SEPTEMBER 2022

"THERE SHOULD ALWAYS HAVE BEEN A BOOK OF BLOCKS."

He melted ice, they said. Great big blocks of ice. Yes, he'd try to melt them on stage. No, there wasn't much else to it, that was the act.

Sometimes, they said, he played tightly-looped music in the background. Oh, and he'd talk to the crowd as he melted the block. A comedy monologue? Not really, they said, he mainly did laborious ice-related pseudo-puns like "I get depriced sometimes."

Listen. In 2010, I wrote a book called *You Are Nothing* about an alternative comedy club called Cluub Zarathustra. Barely a thing had been written about it before, so my approach was to interview a dozen comedians who performed there and a similar number of audience members who witnessed it. "What do you remember about Cluub Zarathustra?" would be my usual way to kick things off and they'd begin with their most potent memories. Quite often, it was the Iceman. And when they didn't start with the Iceman, they'd come to him soon enough.

Everyone felt that the Iceman was "the real deal," one of the thoughtful eccentrics who would never become telly famous but would be remembered fondly by those in the know forever. "The Iceman never had a career plan," said Stewart Lee, dewy-eyed over the purity of '80s alternative variety acts by comparison to today's ambitious young career comics.

I found a 1993 review of the Iceman's Edinburgh Festival show in the *Independent*'s newspaper archive, which taught me that his off-stage name was Anthony Irvine. From this I found via the Internet Movie Database that he'd been in the Jerry Lewis film *Funny Bones*. When I watched the movie he was only in it for a fraction of a second, yet his name came up prominently in the credits. Who was this guy? My friend Ian Macpherson had gigged with him at London's Banana Cabaret. He used the phrase "a memorable block," which introduced me to the vocabulary of the Iceman. (It's never "ice cubes" or even "ice blocks", but always, specifically, "blocks.")

So the Iceman was a legend in both senses of the term. For one, everyone who'd seen him remembered him fondly and could whisper their half-remembered stories about him. For another, there was little about the Iceman online and barely more than footnotes in comedy history books. Like many fringe acts before him, he was, simply, *gone*.

This changed slightly in 2011 when Stewart Lee brought the Iceman out of retirement for two final (ish) blocks at the Royal Festival Hall, a sort of tribute night to the weirder fringe comedy of the 1980s. And then, in 2014, a website popped up called iceblocked.co.uk, which seemed to be run by the Iceman himself. He was painting pictures now, it seemed, but they were all about his original ice-melting act. It was too late for my Cluub Zarathustra book, but I hoped to get in touch with him one day to hear more about his crazy act and his time on the stand-up scene.

One of the things I knew about his act was that he'd take a Polaroid photograph of the block before melting it, as if to honour or commemorate the block. He'd also meticulously number the block like an artwork and record it for posterity in a ledger. I wondered if he still had his photographs and his ledger. It could be a book. It really *should* be a book. It was history!

Eventually, in 2022, I mentioned this fantasy book of blocks to comedy gadfly John Fleming. "I know the Iceman," John said, "he's a lovely man. I'll put you in touch."

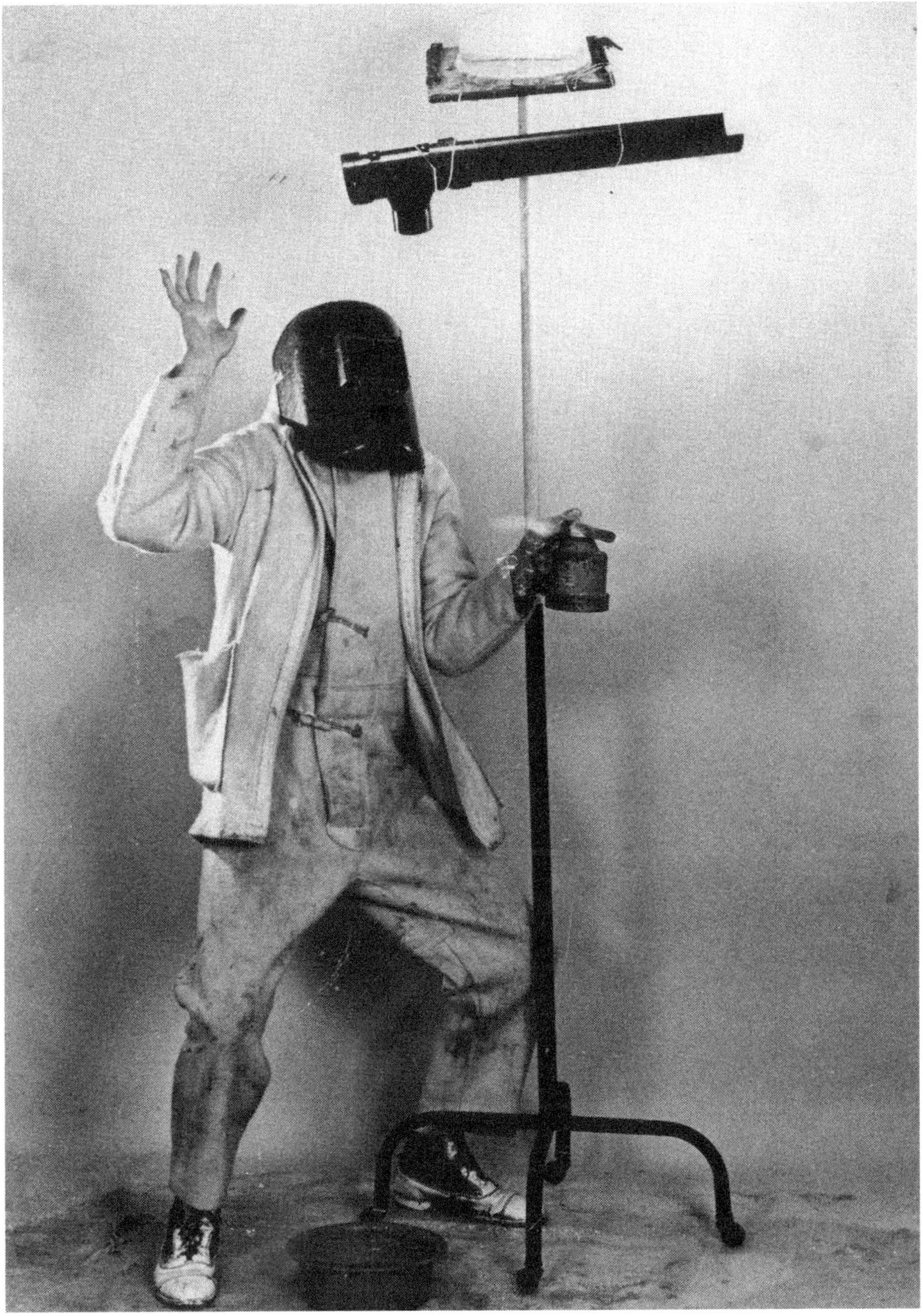

And he did. A couple of days later, I got an email: "Ice to meet you," said the Iceman.

I couldn't believe it. I was communing with the real and actual Iceman. The legend. He was still alive and he was still punning. Maybe he was even still melting.

When I asked if he still had his collection of photographs, he said: "Sadly, Ice only have 56 ice them."

56? Well, it wasn't the thousands I'd been imagining and hoping for but it was, in my opinion, just enough for a little photo book. Most of the blocks had vanished as nature intended, but we could grant immortality to 56 survivors couldn't we?

"There should always have been a book of blocks," the Iceman later told me. He'd made a block book of sorts back in the '80s: "a photocopiced affair. Ice sold three copices."

The Iceman sent me his photographs by courier from his home in Bournemouth to mine in Glasgow. For twelve hours or so, I felt genuine concern that they might get lost on the way. They were, to me, important relics. I would not have been happy to have played a part in their loss. Few others would see it as so important and even the Iceman would probably have laughed it off, told me that he was doomed to transience just like his blocks, but I wanted the blocks and the legend to live on. That was the whole point of the book.

Thankfully, they arrived. And they were wonderful.

When I opened the package, the first thing that struck me was the smell. They reeked! It turns out that twenty-year-old Polaroid photographs, when bundled together, give off a rancid chemical fume. I held my breath and excitedly riffled through them.

The blocks themselves were bigger than I'd imagined and they weren't generally the cube shape I'd imagined either, largely because most of them had been made using buckets and so were cylindrical or trapezoidal in shape.

The first blocks I saw in the pictures were propped up by a rickety wicker gantry. The next ones seemed to be pre-show, still in the freezer. The best ones were shot on-stage with the audience in the background. The audiences were small and they wore a mixture of delighted and bemused expressions (as well as some delightful 1980s and '90s clothes and haircuts), some of them clearly getting the joke and others yet to be convinced.

In addition to the 56 main performance Polaroids, there were a few more recent ones taken in the Iceman's garage—so he *was* still melting—and some great memorabilia. There were newspaper cuttings and promotional photography, my favourite being a black-and-white shot of the Iceman in a mask and boiler suit, reacting with theatrical horror, or perhaps reverence, at the very existence of a block.

Well, we had to do something with these.

We agreed to meet at the Battersea Arts Centre in London for an interview. The interview could run through the book, alongside the photographs. It's often said that the Iceman's act prompted more questions than it answered, but maybe we could get some answers anyway.

Battersea Arts struck me as an apt place to do the interview because the Iceman had played the venue several times in the '80s. Being an arts centre, they'd be sympathetic to our project and maybe give us a space to work in. And, as it happened, they were already hosting our friend Simon Munnery's Edinburgh preview show, so a little reunion would be possible too.

I met the Iceman on the steps of the art centre. He's in his seventies now but I could still recognise the face I'd seen in some of the photographs. He wore a blue artist's smock, sandals, a rusted badge with "Iceman" written on it, and a lanyard proudly displaying the word "aim," which is the new identity he uses for his paintings. He also carried a yellow plastic duck.

The way he carried the duck was disarmingly tender. John Fleming had been right; Anthony Irvine was obviously a lovely man.

I don't like to waste energy before starting an interview, so we started right away. Often, if a subject and I spend time getting to know each other first, details will inevitably come out that go unrecorded, so I set the dictaphone running and we got on with our interview. I learned all about Anthony's pre-ice time in showbusiness, his moment in the alt-alt-comedy spotlight as the Iceman, what happened with *Funny Bones*, his disappearance from the scene, the Royal Festival Hall show, and his more recent paintings.

Anthony explained that the paintings are his current artistic passion but that they're a continuation of his original "performance project" and that some of the paintings are actually versions of moments already captured in the Polaroids. Could we include those in the book, alongside the Polaroids? Yes, he said, this could be an art book. He seemed to like this idea and I did too. The book could be not just a history but a living thing.

Mid-interview, I spotted Simon Munnery in his stetson, checking into the venue. The last time I saw him was in a lockdown-era video chat, which had left me feeling a bit sad and pining for the comedy scene. The last time Anthony saw him, he confided, was twenty years ago. I had no idea it had been so long. I went over to say hello to Simon and, with relish, to reintroduce his old friend.

"Icey-Icey, Baby!" cried Simon on seeing Anthony. It was more than I could have hoped for.

Simon came for some drinks with us after his show. "How many legends are at this table?" said the Iceman. "Well," said Simon, "I count four," generously including me and the duck.

We showed Simon the Polaroids and he cackled audibly on seeing the audience in shot. The sun set, we got drunk, I think I might have told Simon that I loved him before he disappeared into the night. I said a fond farewell to Anthony, and then I slugged myself back to Glasgow to squeeze out another deeply niche comedy history book. And here that book be. The legend lives on!

ROBERT WRINGHAM,
PARTICK
SEPTEMBER 2022.

BLOCK #297

BLOCK #221

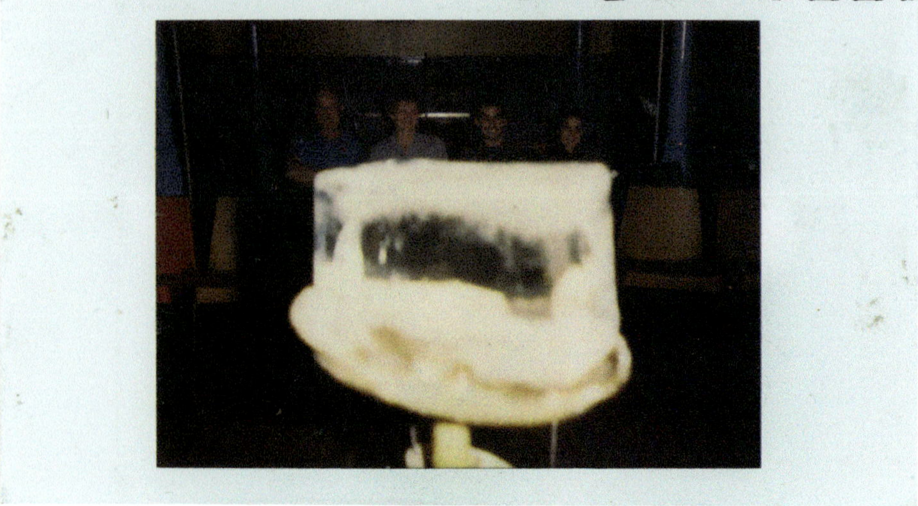

BLOCK #243

BLOCK #535

ORIGINS

BLOCK #1101

Did you really get locked in a freezer as a young man?

It's true and I can remember it vividly. I was working as a milkman in about 1974 and I used to quite like the early mornings. It was at the end of the shift and I was putting unsold milk back in the freezer, and a guy called Spud—he was a very nice bloke really—just shut the door. I remember feeling quite worried after a while because I wasn't quite sure what temperature it was and it was very cold. Though I wasn't getting frostbite or anything I was getting very cold and it was dark. I think I was getting close to panic. You used to see all those public information films about "don't get trapped in a fridge." Fortunately he opened it after a bit. I told him I didn't think it was very funny.

I've done a lot of dangerous jobs. I remember once delivering bread and one of those plastic strips at the door of a fridge almost strangled me. It's quite thick plastic. I was probably nearer death at that point [than when I got shut in the freezer].

I did security in a chicken factory too.

Simon Munnery worked in a chicken factory.

Did he? That's a funny coincidence. I wasn't actually with the chickens, I was more guarding the plant. I'm vegetarian, so of course I felt guilty because I assumed I was supposed to protect the factory from animal rights people so, had they come, I would have let them in. I've also worked with a kangaroo so I have abused animals through ignorance.

Do you think the freezer incident is the origin of the Iceman?

I think it was probably not related, but you never know, subconsciously. I was quite interested in performance art and that attracted me to experimental theatre and multimedia stuff. In Edinburgh in 1979, I did a piece called *Stop It* and I had a repetitive sound, a recording of my own voice saying "Stop it, stop it, stop it," and I think that was possibly the real origin of the Iceman. After that show, which I did with the woman who became the Icewoman, i.e. my wife, Wendy Bave-Christie (she is a lovely dancer who trained at The Place) I thought "right, what's next?" and something called *Melt It* occurred to me.

There's also an idea that you were inspired by a man on Hyde Park Corner?

Yes, literally in Speakers Corner. I got the feeling that this man was doing something slightly profound even if most people thought he was slightly bonkers. I think his commitment struck me. I can't remember what he was talking about, I think it was something about alien worlds, but it was something about the performative nature of it, something fascinating about that. I was conscious at the time that I liked this person. I quite liked the interaction between him and the audience because he got barracked a bit and he dealt with it very calmly and well.

Did your time at boarding school inform your act at all?

I went to a very military school. It was called Haileybury and Imperial Service College. In the old days they produced civil servants for the East India Company but in my day it was just very much a boys' boarding school and the houses were named after military commanders like Allenby. I do think this this was probably when I went into my own world because I wasn't enjoying it much and perhaps, in a funny way, that made me more creative. I mean, I went through all the motions and had the education of sorts but in a funny way the suppression of it all gave me some creativity somehow. I think going into myself was an act of survival really. I wasn't very happy there but I didn't quite have the nouse to run away.

WENDY

TEARS

I was a fag. You know about that? An older boy could tell me what to do. I didn't suffer any abuse though, fortunately. Then again, I got six of the best from the headmaster once so maybe I did.

What did you parents think of your career choices?

Probably my father was slightly bemused about it, but I don't think he ever saw the ice act. My mother was more open to my creative ideas. She'd gone to Bedales and been a dancer with Margaret Morris. I think my father felt I should go into law or something like that. My home life was traditional but in a funny way creative and radical in a way. I had three amusing older brothers who were more dominant than me, so as well as at school, on holidays, I would retreat into my own ideas in the family setting as well. There was non-stop talk of politics in part because my dad was a politician. Although, it was a secure and loving family so I mustn't malign it.

Did you go into acting before you were drawn into performance art? Were you an actor first?

After a fashion. I did a play in this very building [Battersea Arts Centre]. I actually went to university for three years, so I'm quite over-educated, and then I had a few more years mucking about, well not "mucking about" but doing quite a lot of street theatre and stuff. I belonged to a street theatre group in Penge called Shoestring Theatre. I remember the first show we did was at Clapham. There's a big pub in the middle and we did something like a bad version of *Dad's Army*. I was a gormless Private called Private Parts and we did sort of military things. We made a lot of money from collecting. We did the Rolling Stones at Knebworth [in 1976].

I think this all led to a desire for a more formal training so, in 1977, I went to the Welsh College of Music and Drama. I have no

Welsh blood, I'm Scottish in fact, but I think it was the cheapest one and I was self-financing. I did a year's postgraduate course in drama, training as an actor, but I didn't really fit in. I did a lot of shows but I began to realise I wasn't really an actor. I remember in our last assessment piece I went up a very high ladder and dropped a big television. Apparently it annoyed the assessor who thought I was just showing off.

So I was doing performance art when they wanted me to act. I left a dent in that theatre for years to come! I did a few mediocre jobs as an actor, some of them not entirely mediocre, and in this very building I did an experimental touring production called *Rational*, as opposed to National, *Theatre*. And a guy called Peter Godfrey wrote a play called *Falling* and we toured around all winter. The set was quite simple but very nice with these cocoons that knocked over these cardboard boxes at the end. I played a character called Chewy and I had a lot of ritualistic movements a bit like Tai-chi before Tai-chi was popular here. People used to quite like that character because he had a very physical basis. Ironically, because I was anxious to work, I got into variety shows. I did a touring cabaret act called Jo, Jac & Joni whose original people are in the London Palladium hall of fame. They were three pretend musicians who'd come on and you'd think they were going to play but then they do a lot of visual gags like Laurel and Hardy. For example I had a bassoon with a cigarette at the top of it and the other guy had a clarinet, but he takes the top off the clarinet and he uses it to light my cigarette. They were all prop-heavy visual gags like that. We were quite big in East Germany before the wall came down. It was the only time we ever had fans at the door asking for photos and we had a 32-piece orchestra behind us.

CURIOUS YELLOW

BLOCK #171

Please tell me about your work with the kangaroo.

I worked in a circus with a six-foot kangaroo. In fact I shared a truck with it, the poor beast. These experiences are all leading to the ice block, I think. The kangaroo was called Skippy of course and I was a clown with a guy called Fillipo. It was a huge circus called *Circo Moira Orfei.* It had everything. I don't know if this is even allowed now, but there were tigers and elephants, the lot. Three or four times a day we went into the arena and did a routine where we'd knock each other out in a proper boxing ring and then I'd go and get the kangaroo by its tail. I remember vividly my very first entry into the circus ring, guiding the Kangaroo on by its tail from behind towards the boxing ropes set up in the centre. One of the Moroccan roustabouts tripped me up with his foot, as a joke. It was was easy to do as I was wearing huge clown shoes. I collapsed onto the rear of the Kangaroo, sprawling over its tail. It was my first big laugh! It was a very loud laugh because it was completely spontaneous because it was done *to* me. Anyway, I bring the kangaroo on, and I hardly like to confess this, but I dug it in the ribs to get it excited and slightly angry and I gave him his mating call, which I was trained to do, so he would get cross and excited. It's terrible really. He would fight and try and get hold of the other clown round the neck with his forepaws and then kick him. To kick him to death would be his aim. My job would be to [act like a] referee but also, if he was really angry, to release the forepaws which are weaker than the hindlegs. So I had a double role, to save Fillipo's life every day and to irritate the kangaroo. He had boxing gloves on, the poor thing, and it was a really wonderful act except, in retrospect, it obviously wasn't nice for the animals. This was probably the last authentic boxing kangaroo act.

Fillipo clearly trusted you if you were saving his life every night.

He was more like a proper clown, but unfortunately it all ended when my [*laughs*] wife and I had a quarrel in the auditorium while we were watching the rest of the circus after my bit. We'd just married and [she felt] that I'd left her for a kangaroo. There was quite a dangerous acrobatic performance going on and we were having this quarrel, a heated discussion, about love because she naturally thought I'd abandoned her for the circus. She said "you don't know what love is" and the acrobats lost their balance. We literally had to run away from a circus. It was Christmas Day in fact. In *Torino,* Italy. I left my unicycle behind.

I was quite resentful but she probably saved my life because it was quite a dangerous life. In fact, the kangaroo was trying to go for me once and it was Fillipo who got me out of the way. In fact, his father had died in the ring and I was his father's understudy. Not very good really, but it was exciting. In my own ignorance I couldn't help being excited because it was a mammoth circus with trapeze artists and monkeys and horses, the lot.

It's very romantic. It's the kind of thing a lot of clown-minded comedians would be envious of today, I think.

Romantic, sort of, yes. I've been a genuine clown with makeup and the lot. It was quite extraordinary really. I lived in the truck with the kangaroo. There was a partition between us and there were all sorts of things happening next door. We got a baby kangaroo. Outside my door there, I do not exaggerate, was an elephant swinging [its trunk] around all night and apparently it had killed some people. There was also the tigers but I felt particularly sorry for them because they were going around and around in this small space all night.

BLOCK #179

BLOCK #186

Tell me a bit more about your time in street theatre.

I was in various random groups. I was in one called Theatre of Lies and we used to get together for specific events and festivals, the names of which I can hardly remember. There was Andrew Bailey and a guy called Simon [not Munnery] who drove a hearse which could convert into a stage. We used to get people taking their hats off as we passed. Simon was very tall, I was sort of middle and Andew... I don't know if you know Andrew Bailey?

I think I do! Is he bald?

He is bald. He's another bizarre guy, a bit like me, slightly off-beat.

Yes, he does wonderful prop comedy. I've seen him do a brilliant thing called Ministry of Toys and there's his bingo routine where he blows the balls through tubes.

We did a lot of stuff together, I can't even remember when. It might have been after my so-called formal training, I don't know. I've always liked that sort of thing to be honest. I never really became, sort of, a proper actor [*laughs*]. I think that's down to a lack of talent in my case or maybe a lack of discipline. All those lines! But I was quite good.

BLOCK #193

BLOCK #202

BLOCK #236

BLOCK #179

BLOCK #208

BLOCK #192

THE ACT

CHAIN

When did you first perform as the Iceman?

I can remember the first block. It was at this place called Crazy Larry's in Chelsea in about 1983. This new club had started and people like Rory Bremner were doing it, so I just did it. It was in clubs from the word go.

Did you use the Iceman name straight out of the gate?

Somebody gave it to me. But quite quickly, shortly after that first block. My original name for the act was *Melt It* but the Iceman is an easier name, a moniker sort of thing.

How long did you usually do? Ten minutes, twenty minutes? A couple of hours?

[*laughs*] Twenty minutes. But I did an open air one in Covent Garden for example, which was an all-day one. People used to come back to see how it was doing.

I must say though, that the performance in a sense started from when the water was put into the fridge or freezer, continuing on the journey to the venue. Deep!

The performance continued after the stage performance ended, in the sense that the journey was maintained afterwards, the block still being at least partially intact sometimes, to a known or unknown end. Deep!

With commercial bought blocks, the performance started with the telephone order for the work in the refrigeration plant but really began properly with the first meeting of the Block with the Iceman. Deep!

Did you see yourself as a comedian or a performance artist or something else?

In the beginning I felt very much a performance artist. And that was different. I had this opportunity to share my thoughts and pain etc., and that was slightly therapeutic for me. I mean, people found it funny, so it was the funny side of intellectual performance art, but because people found it funny I moved over into the comic. And then, I think, later on I became more verbal because I couldn't fill a twenty-minute spot with just flinging ice about.

Wait, so it was a silent act to begin with?

Yes. Well, I made involuntary sounds reflecting my extreme efforts. But it was silent in that it was almost completely visual. And when I look back, those are my favourite blocks, those early ones because they were totally pure. Totally, like, demonstrating what I was feeling, with props and ice.

Was the nudge into comedy because you were doing something earnestly and people were laughing because of the inherent humour of it? Or was it just because comics like Simon Munnery kept inviting you to play their gig?

I like your word "earnestly" because I think that's what did move people in a way as well as amuse them. As well as amuse them, it moved them emotionally. Because I *was* earnest. It was like "I've *got* to do this block" but, as Simon used to say, the irony was that it would melt anyway. So that's the comedy of it I suppose. It's all about failure but out of that failure we have success because ultimately it will melt, even if it's just in the street outside. I was the catalyst really, speeding it up.

I think the early blocks were a form of attention seeking, I suppose, but also there was a therapeutic element, I think.

One of your first approaches to melting the block is just to breathe on it. I always thought that was a good gag. It tells them what your intention is and also that it's going to escalate.

And also it's interactive because you can get the audience to breathe on it too. It's funny how childlike audiences are. As long as you lead them, it's amazing how they join in. It's because they're sympathetic. So I'd get them all blowing towards the ice.

LONG ICE

BLOCK #191

Later, it became more structured and there were even a few verbal jokes, like, really bad ones and people would laugh because it was so bad. And so then it was more about filling a twenty-minute spot in comedy clubs. But it never quite lost the anarchy of the early years, which sometimes annoyed people but on the whole amused them.

Tell me a bit more about the escalation.

Yes, escalation was the name of the game. In a strange way it was quite structured. Basically, I would come on, introduce myself with something like "Hi, I'm the Iceman, I'm a nice man" to get a laugh and because I had all my props I was already getting a visual impact, and they'd all drop and be all over the place. I would build the structure and then I would get the ice block out and put it on the structure, and that was usually the first collapse! That was the beginning. Miraculously, the block would stay up eventually. And then I went through the different escalations.

I'd start with breath and then I had a magnifying glass, then I had a deicer spray mounted on my head like a hat made of bandages with an attachment. Then I sprayed it and I'd usually pretend that it had all gone in my eyes, which it often did really so I had lots of blindness situations, staggering about.

After that, there was friction, then candles, then money. I'd try to get money from the audience, which I'd use to chip away at the block but really it was supposed to be a bribe to get the block to melt.

There was salt, which I'd rub into the block, and then I'd move on quite quickly to the hammer and chisel, which is quite radical and would often split the block. This would be seen as a partial success and I'd say "the iceman is an ice-breaker!" or something.

Then I would shoot the block with my stage gun, which

looked and sounded good, but there wasn't an actual bullet so it wouldn't really do anything. Then that's when I got the pyrotechnics out.

I had a sort of pod which I'd put on the block and the audience always seemed a bit worried because it looked dangerous. I would fire it and it was quite a good little explosion, but I don't think there was much destruction, it was just visual.

There was the blowtorch too. The blowtorch was the most dangerous because I'd already sprayed the deicer. In small clubs it had a big effect.

As well as escalation, a theme was struggle. I'd be knocking things over, blinding myself, shooting the duck, scaring people with my incompetence and explosives. I could never get the candles to light, things like that. I'd say "this candle is getting on my wick," so dispersed between all these acts of failure would be these terrible verbal puns. There was also electricity involved so it probably was really dangerous and I didn't really realise it.

In a strange way, it did build to a climax. But then it took a long time to move it all off-stage, which probably annoyed some comedians. Or they had to work in my mess.

There was real danger as well as the illusion of danger?

It's completely unbelievable when you think about it now. I was quite lucky really. I mean, I deafened myself. I have let pyrotechnics go off in my face. I remember having a dustbin once with a sort of bang effect and it was so loud in a small club that, as well as deafening myself, I'm afraid I might have deafened a few people in the front row. That was in Bracknell. It surprised me. It was the biggest bang you've ever heard, louder than a wartime bomb. I wasn't really a specialist. I used to buy all these things and then they used to take me by surprise.

BLOCK #198

BLOCK #199

Tell me about some of your injuries.

They're largely mental.

Otherwise, quite minor. Toes are vulnerable, with the block falling off its structure. And falling over. I used to fall over a lot. Deicer in my eyes. Scratches, cuts, splinters. They were all minor but bad enough to demonstrate suffering; something taken from me by the block.

No frostbite?

No, but you'd have to be careful because if you kept your hand on too long you'd lose some skin. In that way, I respected the block.

BLOCK #297

BLOCK #203

BLOCK #738

BLOCK #215

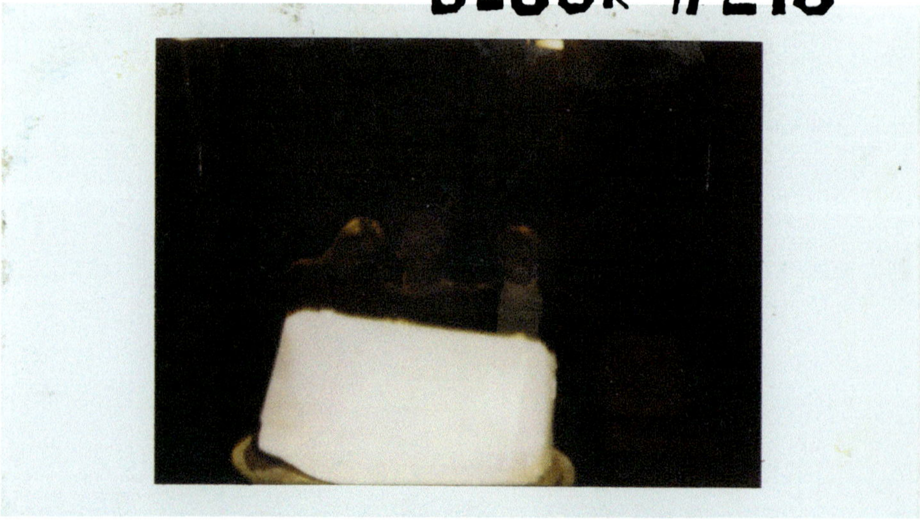

BLOCK #189

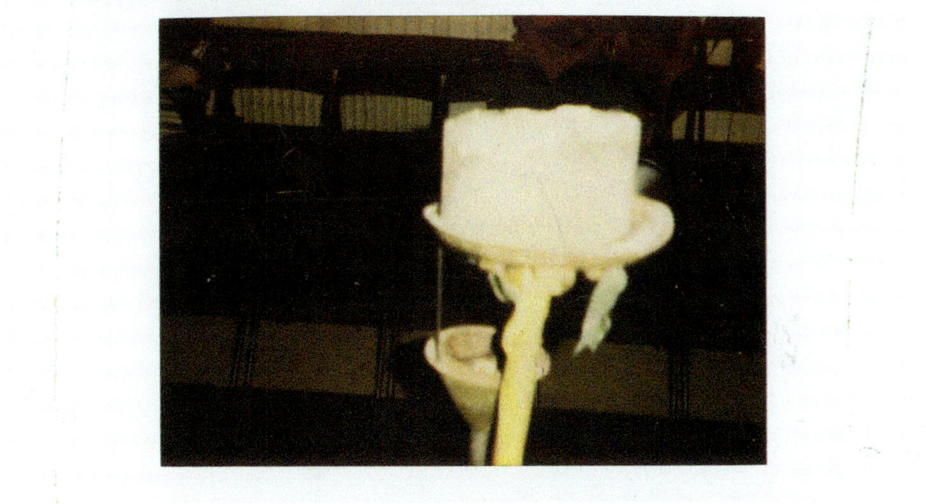

BLOCK #17

THE DUCK

THE DUCK

What did you do with the duck?

I was put up in a hotel in Southampton for this terrible TV show [called *Prove It*]. [Our mutual friend] John Fleming was there, I remember. In this hotel there was this duck. It was hotel property and I took it. The idea was to use it in my act but it became more and more a central motif. I'd spend some time setting up my system and then I'd introduce them to the ice duck, my "iceprentice," and I'd say "I'm going to put him in dry duck." You've got the right sense of humour for it but most people were groaning! And the idea was that, as the ice melted, the duck would float. But in fact, the water hardly ever got into the bucket, it got everywhere else. At the end of the performance, I'd often shoot the duck. I had a proper stage gun and I'd pretend to shoot the block only the bullet ricochets off and it kills the duck. My end line was "oh fuck, I've killed the duck" and then I drop a feather and say "what a downer." So you can see how bad this act was!

It's wonderful.

The duck in a sense had a practical purpose. It was meant to be a gauge of how effective I was being, and occasionally it actually would float and pop up near the top of the bucket, but also the idea was to have a friend and... someone I could rely on. To this day, I feel affection towards it, and I don't just treat it like a plastic duck. In fact, I put it at the front of the bus on the way to meet you today so it could have a nice view. I noticed when he didn't have a very good view and I adjusted it.

You can't get ducks like your one anymore. I was looking for one for an unrelated project.

Really?

You know I'm writing a novel but what I didn't say is that it's called Rub-a-Dub-Dub. It's about bathtime so I thought we could put a rubber duck on the cover. But rubber ducks don't look like that anymore. I wanted a 1970s-style one. And you can't get 'em.

That's extraordinary because I often rubbed the block with a friction implement or some sandpaper, saying "rub-a-dub, rub-a-dub," shaking my cheeks monstrously above the duck. It always got quite a laugh.

I'm extra-glad I gave my book that title then.

I wrote to the hotel in Southampton to ask if they wanted compensation or the duck returned but they didn't write back. It might have been left by another guest, I suppose.

I had a duck just like that one as a child, but it was the big one in a set of three. There was a middle-sized one and a little baby one. So your duck has lost its original colleagues.

I think I played on the idea of loneliness. I'd sort of imply that life would let you down but the duck doesn't. So I feel a strange friendship with the duck. He also appears in quite a lot of my paintings. One thing I'm getting good at in painting is the duck because I paint him quite often. Though he was actually quite a late addition to the act; I'd always be adding things. I don't say that I was necessarily trying to improve it but I was continually trying to put more elements in.

BLOCK #535

THE DUCK WATCHES

BLOCKFUL 7

BLOCK #196

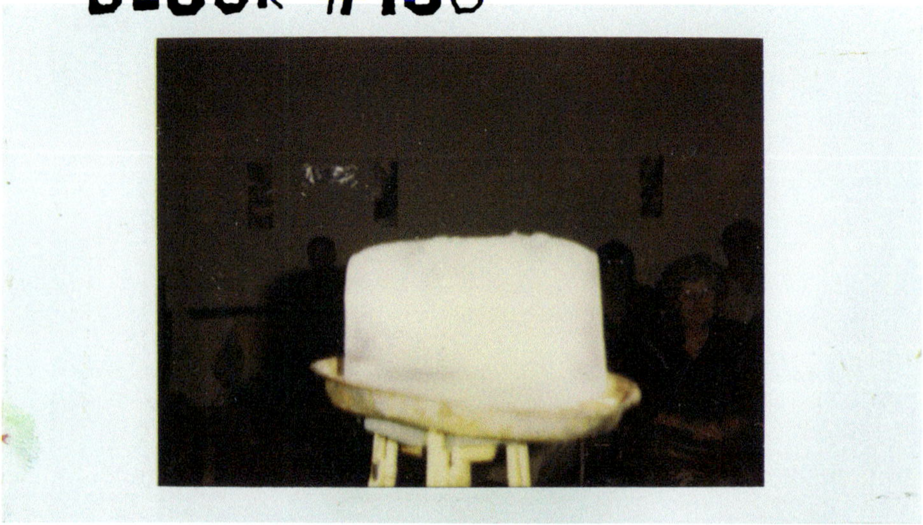

BLOCK #191

BLOCK #271

BLOCK #259

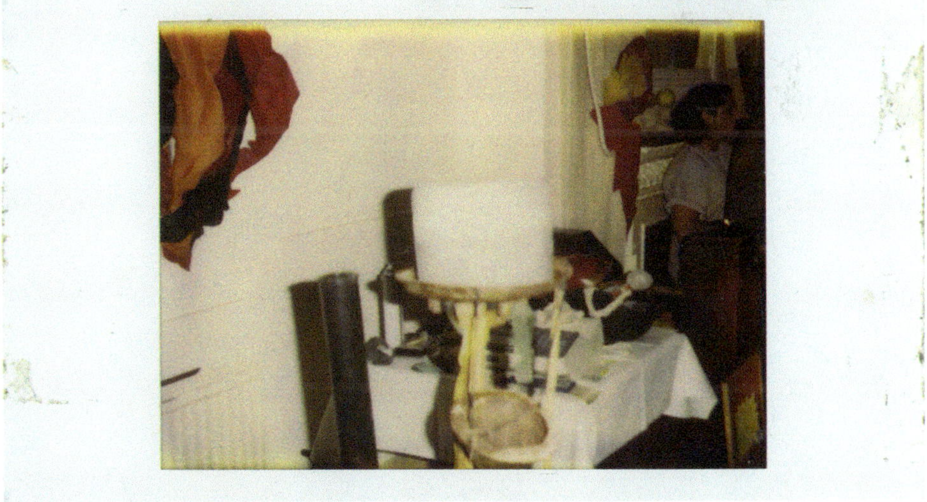

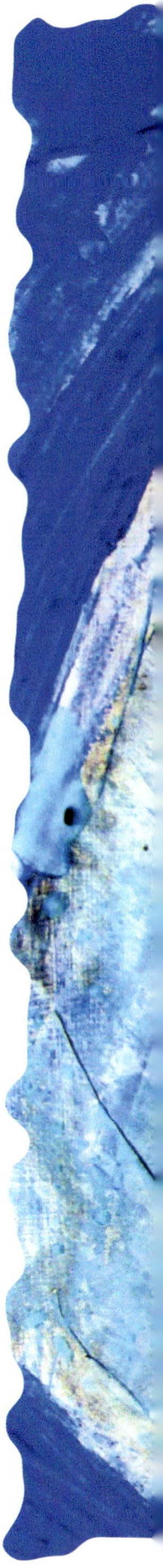

THE LOOP

BLOCK #857

BLOCK #202

Tell me about the loop.

It's called *I Can't Realise You Love Me* by Duke Ellington.

How and why did you choose that record and why did you loop it? Were you actively trying to annoy people?

Funnily enough, at the Royal Festival Hall show [in 2011], a guy came up to me and said "CAN YOU PLEASE TURN THAT OFF?" He was quite aggressive, but he was surprised when I was so polite with my "oh, sorry, is this annoying you?"

The idea was to have some background noise while the visual stuff was going on really. But rather than have a whole song, I somehow created my own loop with lots of repetitive "I can't realise you love me"s. It's a very old-fashioned, sort of constricted sound. I can't realise you love meeeeeeee!

Did you think the song was funny before you employed it?

I think I did but it's even funnier when it's repeated. But somehow it struck a chord with me because one element of the block was about love and love's demise—*demice*—so somehow I quite like the idea that I can't believe I was ever loved or worthy of love, that sort of thing. It contributes to the pathos of the thing.

And I had storm sound effects on it, which was quite dramatic. I was never very technological, so in a way the rough nature of the tape is quite nice too. And then I got my wife, at the end of it, to say "I don't love you" so after ages and ages of "I can't realise you love me," you get that. At one performance, the "I don't love you" came in at precisely the right moment when the act stopped. That got a huge pathos laugh and it never happened again, before or since.

I just like the loop as part of the overall event. I suppose I was trying to have a sort of multimedia event really, not just the block. Different levels, a bit like Shakespeare, how the groundlings enjoyed the comedy, the intellectuals got something else, and the spiritual people got something else, and the questioning people got the "Deep! Deep!"

On one occasion, a Buddhist lady came up and said "it's all about karma isn't it?" and she was deadly serious. I went along with it and said "yeah, I suppose it is." Then I realised it was.

It was meant to be a bit poignant but I was conscious that it was quite annoying. It drowned a lot of my verbals but it's quite funny having that going on very steadily while I'm quite active. So it gave me a sort of anchor in a funny way.

I read somewhere that there was a block you just allowed to melt?

That was the Covent Garden one I mentioned. Oh, but there was also a clifftop block in Bournemouth. I just left it on the clifftop. Although that didn't really have an audience. Just me, my camera, some seagulls, and a few random people who were trying to find somewhere to wee.

Do you do that often? Just melt a block for your own amusement?

No, but I quite like the beauty of ice blocks. This TikTok one I did, I froze it just for the video. Having frozen it, I took some photographs which I thought were quite interesting. That TikTok one was a bit indulgent, I suppose. Nice to do sometimes. I usually do a block with a purpose.

Did you try to convey a sense of impatience in the act? Keeping in mind that it was going to melt anyway.

Yes, impatience. Or more desperation really. That amused people. There was no particular ability about the act. The ice would normally fall down quite quickly, then I would spend some time lifting it up again.

Later on, I had quite a delicate structure. I had bamboo and to my amazement it stayed up longer

BLOCK #206

BLOCK #215

than normal. I went through so many changes but the bamboo was quite interesting because it's quite strong but delicate at the same time. I think the unpredictability of it was nice, both for me and the audience. But it was about struggle really. And the struggle was genuine!

And the struggle starts before the act because it's quite an effort sometimes with blocks of ice. To actually get them to the venue in a frozen state. And also afterwards it was quite a struggle getting home without much money and carrying all my props and stuff.

How did you make the blocks?

Primarily in my own freezer or fridge. But for bigger shows I'd go to a really friendly company called Eskimo Ice. They were somewhere in South London and they made really big blocks. I'd use them for TV shows.

Have you ever adulterated a block or are they always pure water?

Have I ever used it to reduce my sexual drives? No, I think I quite like the purity of the block. But occasionally I have experimented by putting something in it, maybe even the duck, but it never felt quite right, not being true to the idea of the block. I have a strange loyalty to blocks. I experimented with colour sometimes, with dye and paint and little objects, but I always went back to the pristine block. Deep!

SMOKE GETS IN YOUR ICES

BLOCK #1101

BLOCK #217

DIAGRAIM

BLOCK #282

BLOCK #287

BLOCK #284

BLOCK #283

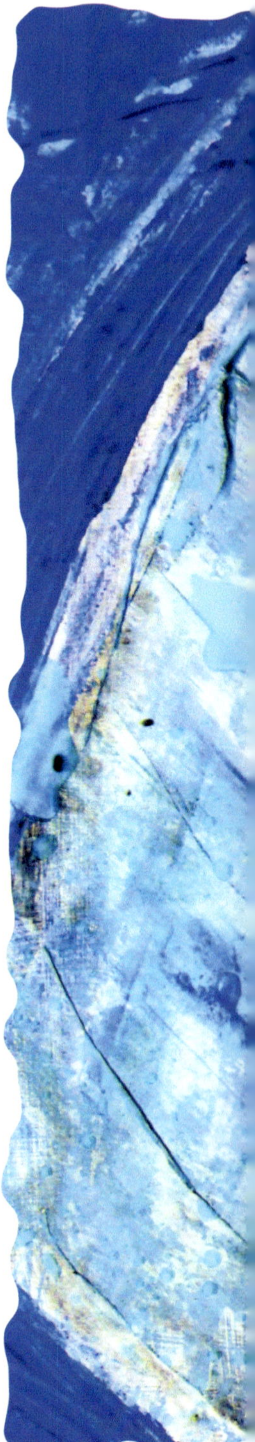

DOCUMENTATION

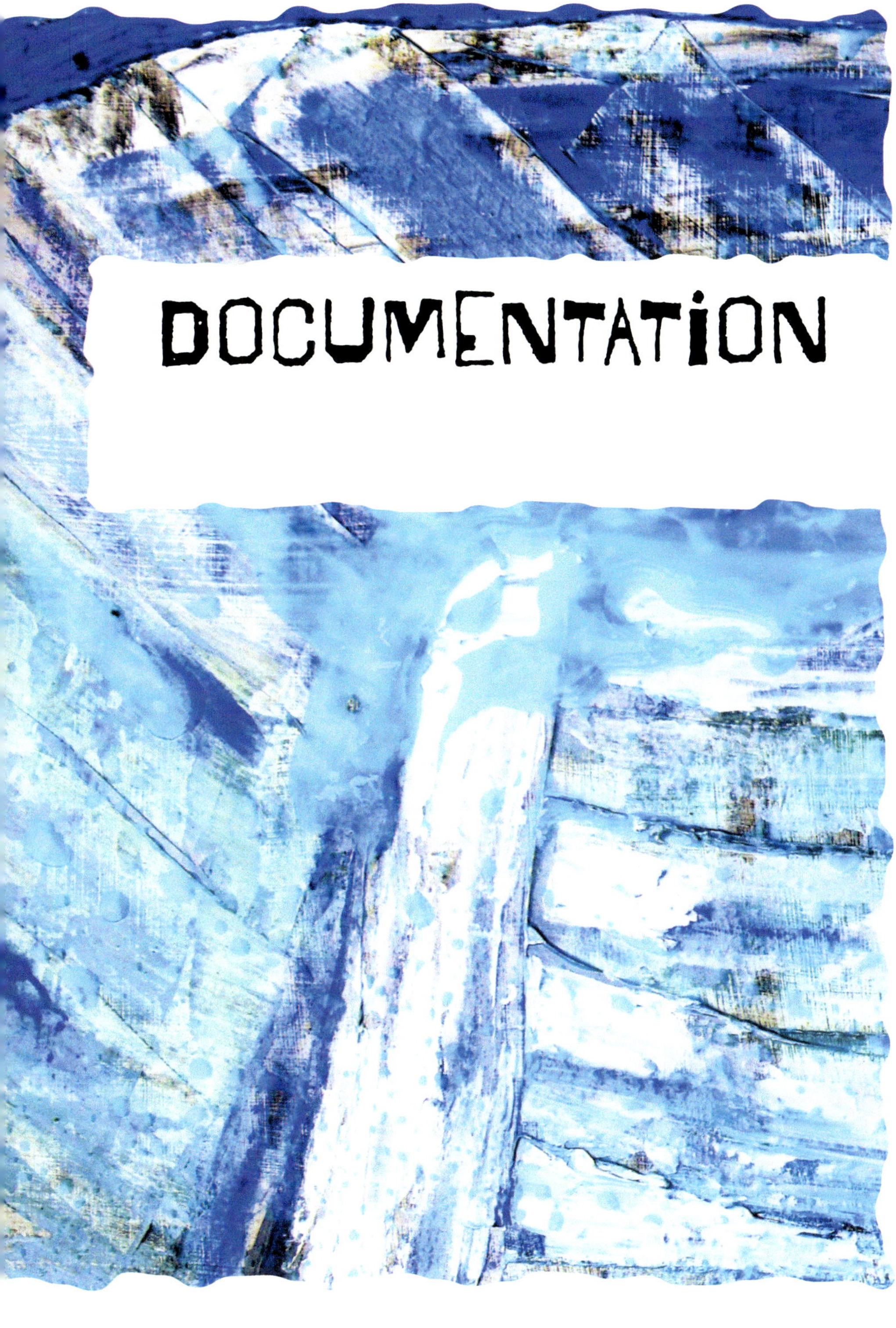

BLOCK #221

The documentation of each block is very entertaining to me. I thought it would be wonderful if you still had all of the documentation.

And I let you down a little bit, didn't I? Because I only had about 56 of the Polaroids left.

But that's enough really.

It's quite arbitrary what survives really. I think I did have a phase where, unlike me, I was very meticulous and then I think I rather lost it all, just let it go. In a way I regret not keeping more records but it's just the way it goes. But 56 is not bad and there might be a few faxed copies out there; I don't know if people kept them. That was quite a feature of the so-called act. A very bad, old-fashioned fax copy, on fax paper, came out and I signed it and I would usually sell some of them during the act or afterwards.

How much did you get for them?

Not very high amounts. I mean, ten pounds would be good. Single figures mostly.

I always had a vision of you keeping a record, recording the blocks in a ledger or something.

I did have a ledger, which I chucked. I became self-destructive, I think, of my memorabilia. Maybe it was frustration, or maybe it was an attempt to let it all be a bit more open, to not be so anal about it, to say "let's just see how it all develops." But I think maybe it was more out of a sense of dissatisfaction.

But I quite like how it's a bit more open now and I've got paintings. Some people don't know whether they're paintings of actual blocks or if they're imaginary. In the paintings, the blocks live on. The photographs happened as a result of the blocks and the paintings are an extension.

BLOCK #991

BLOCK #991

BLOCK #223

FUMBLE

BLOCK #179

BLOCK #350

BLOCK #281

BLOCK #283

THE ICEMAN ON TV

THE TUBE

You did a bit of telly.

It was mainly variety shows. I did a thing called *Prove It* [in 1988] with Chris Tarrant. He got quite cross with me really. He said "this act is shit!"

It rings a bell. Was it a sort of talent show thing?

It was, I think. It was a bit embarrassing really.

I did a Noel Edmonds Christmas Show in 1985 and I made a little mountain of 24 really big blocks by arranging them in a triangular formation. They probably lasted til summer. And I got a special fridge! I came out of it, an exploding fridge. But the fridge didn't have a back on it so it lost its impact and it was just like coming out of a box. But I wasn't going to pay some pyrotechnics expert to put something together with a fridge even though I had quite a good expense account for the TV show. Someone called Mike Smith, Noel Edmonds' sidekick, lowered himself from a helicopter to interview me. It was quite bizarre really. But I always made the point that I was concentrating on my work and that the interview was a distraction.

That reminds me of how you'd sometimes make an entrance in your stage act with a fridge door obscuring you.

Gosh, I'd forgotten about that, yes, I did. I think it probably was the leftover door from the Noel Edmonds thing. I'd forgotten about that! Hiding behind the fridge door like a shield! I didn't do that very often, maybe only about ten times.

It's like you have this central premise of melting the ice and then things build around that.

It's never been the same. That's one of the things I like about it. Maybe I should have made it more compact but, I mean, for example, quite early on, I experimented with having a block on my head. I had a contraption on my head, built on a hard hat, for a pub show, but that was quite difficult. It's been through a lot of phases. I've never really sat still with it, it's always changing. In later years, it became slightly more predictable because I did a show at the Edinburgh Fringe [in 1993] where I did more or less the same structure.

Did you do TV adverts?

I had a spell, I'm afraid, where I did TV commercials, and I used to get quite a few because I was so in-your-face. Whereas you'd have these actors coming in and saying "what is my motivation to drink this lager," and I would come in and get on with it.

***Did you enjoy being on [music show]* The Tube?**

It was pre-duck, so around 1986 or '87. I met Morrissey, not properly, but I remember there was a teenage boy who got a special prize to interview Morrissey. I don't recall actually speaking to Morrissey. I might have nodded to him, but whether he nodded back is another matter.

The main person I met was Jools Holland. It was among all of his bands but I had a block there and I basically did a sample version of my act and he interviewed me during it. I remember that he picked up on the idea of time. He said "it's about time, isn't it?" and of course that's one of the things. Deep! So I went along with that. But I was a fish out of water really because it was very much a music thing. But I remember having my own dressing room and feeling rather special.

Jools does have time for his absurdist performance art, doesn't he? I think he's friends with Reeves and Mortimer?

Yes, and he was friends with Malcolm Hardee. I remember being on with him when he was a compère. He used to step in for Malcolm in Greenwich [at the Tunnel Club] so I met him a few times. I even played an accordion in a restaurant where he was having a meal.

So I can't remember much about *The Tube* but it was very

BLOCK #235

UPLIFTED

exciting to be in a TV studio. I had organised the block myself. It's always quite real, I don't pretend. I actually do things for the block. The block always has an experience.

There was a live audience so I kept going throughout and maybe they picked up on my performance, but I was really only exposed when Jools came to interview me. But I quite like that. Why do it just for the TV cameras?

What did you do on Jameson Tonight? Was it recorded at the Windmill Theatre?

We did an absurd routine called Secret Transfer. Two secret agents meet in a very small cubicle. One is laden down with cutlery packed into huge coat, the other (me) with gravel packed into a similar coat. In the process of the inefficient transfer, everything ends up on the floor including the wooden cubicle. Chaos. Barbara Windsor liked it.

BLOCK #308

BLOCK #228

BLOCK #223

BLOCK #206

BLOCK #239

BLOCK #857

FAILURE AND PREMATURE MELT

TUNNEL

How is the act about failure? Because to me it looks quite successful in that you always melt the block.

Well, the block is practically always still there at the end. In one form or another.

I assumed it was always water by the end of the act!

No, but there was water at the beginning of the act once. The day of the premature melt. It was a hot day in the Blackwall Tunnel and I noticed a lot of water running down the bus aisle. I didn't really realise it was my water. So when I got onto the stage and I turned the bucket over, it just, sort of, *was* water.They were quite rough at the Tunnel Palladium so I just said something like, "oh, I can go home now."

Without the block I was completely superfluous. But that was the only time it happened that way.

How did you fill your ten minutes?

I didn't. I just went prematurely.

Did they heckle you off? Because they were horrible there weren't they?

They were horrible sometimes but on a good night you could win them over. The oddness of the Iceman event kept them onside to an extent. But I think they were actually quite amused by the premature melt. I'd had worse times there.

Malcolm Hardee pissed on my penguin once. I had this endearing little furry penguin as part of my set. Malcolm came on, as was his way, to upstage me by doing a wee. He weed everywhere but the penguin bore the brunt of it. Malcolm probably saved my life because the audience had become riled up, perhaps by the innocent penguin. I have done a painting of the incident in which the famous Hardee balls are graphically displayed.

But on the day of the premature melt, they just loved that it had melted, I think, and I went before any trouble started.

So did they understand your act? Surely you can only find that funny if you already know what was supposed to happen.

That's an interesting question. I'm not quite sure what they were expecting. I suppose, after a bit, I got a slight reputation so that people knew of the idea, but only on the basis of "this man melts blocks of ice and he's crazy." I had a slight following who took it more seriously. I think it started at Glastonbury.

I remember being at one of Simon Munnery's gigs and I had a small following from Glastonbury and they were all going "Deep! Deep!"

Is that where "Deep! Deep!" started? At Glastonbury?

In 1990, yes. I also used to have a Question and Answer session at the end. I'd say "the iceman is a *wice* man" and I'd say "any questions?" and they'd say something like "why?" and I'd give a mysterious answer like "because it's necessary" and I'd get them to say "Deep! Deep!" That would become a running gag for the end of the act and sometimes they were almost waiting for it. It's another example of change. I don't know if I was getting bored but I'd keep fiddling with the concept.

What else happened at Glastonbury?

I had a block go missing for a bit. I think it was hippies. It was the drugs. Their drugs, I mean, not mine. They just needed some ice, man. They needed it badly, they couldn't wait.

On the subject of change, I think the main change was visual to verbal. It became more entertaining and I'd sing songs like *Edelweiss* and *Cheek to Cheek*. I had proper singing lessons for a bit and I became quite a good singer. I remember a lady coming up and saying "I love you singing." She was from Germany and I couldn't tell if she was taking the piss.

BLOCK #236

BLOCK #237

You should have released a record. The Iceman Sings.

I know, I didn't do it enough really.

Did you ever sing with Arthur Smith?

No, but he was always a nice guy. Reminded me of Sid James. I once lamented that his crowd had enjoyed so much more success than me and he said "you had your moments." I always remembered that phrase because that's true, I had my moments.

You have many comedian fans by the sound of it. Mark Thomas for example.

I sold him a painting, yes. And Mike Myers! His comedian friend Neil Mullarkey says that Mike Myers still talks about it.

He's one of the biggest comedians on the planet and he's a fan of yours.

Had I been more of a clever person I could probably have done something with that. He did the circuit before he became famous. I was on with him at Banana Cabaret in Balham and he knows the number. It was an early block. It was Block 69. And he refers to me as *Melt It 69*. I don't really know him; I probably met him without even realising it.

MELTWATER

BLUE

BLOCK #240

BLOCK #235

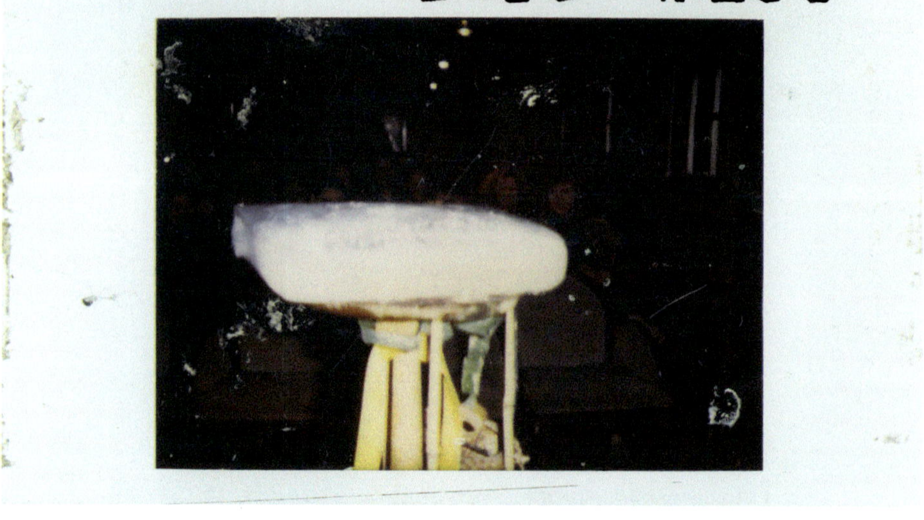

BLOCK #199

BLOCK #228

CLUBS AND GIGS (1986-1997)

BLOCK #240

How do they relate to you in the clubs? Do comedians see you as one of their own or as an outside figure? Did they love your act and say "oh, the Iceman's on tonight"?

I'm not sure. I think I always had some people in my corner like Stewart Lee and Co. who felt I was up to something. I obviously have some distance from normal comedy. Some of the straighter comedians liked me. Ivor Dembina, who is very nice, booked me for the Red Rose Club quite a few times. I remember Mark Kelly, quite a political comedian, said to me once that Ivor had asked "is he genuine about it?" This was interesting to me because I thought I was particularly genuine and Mark said "you seem to be genuine because of all the effort you put in" and the fact that I didn't really court success in the usual sense of the word.

I think that's to your great credit.

Thank you. I think they thought I was a bit outsiderish probably. I'm more like a novelty act. They were concentrating on their verbal, "will I get laughs?" stuff.

You performed at Cluub Zarathustra a few times. Was it the London or the Edinburgh edition?

London. The first time I went there, there had been some IRA trouble. I got stopped outside the club by a huge police van with about fifty policemen in it and they were suspicious of me. I used to drive a small white van, which must have looked suspicious to them. They quickly established that I was genuine but the funny thing was that they didn't look in my boot. Had they looked in my boot I could have been shot.

Bombs?

[*laughing*] I had guns! My stage guns. They were very real looking. And worse, there were cables and what looked like high-powered explosives. I remember thinking how lucky that was really.

I didn't do that many blocks at Zarathustra really but I remember that there was a special energy there and I liked the people there, Simon Munnery and Co. It reminded me slightly of a more sophisticated version of another club called Open Heart Cabaret where it had been acceptable to do a lot of different things.

Yes, traditional stand-up was forbidden.

Exactly. I remember using my fax machine there. I think I faxed a few blocks to people. I just remember the ambience was sympathetic and I felt at home there.

There were quite a few famous people in the audience, unexpectedly. Gary Oldman, I think. And I remember Simon's thing, very dictatorial, "you are all worms," sort of thing. It was very funny.

How did you first get involved? Did Simon bring you in?

I think I literally got a phonecall. Simon called me up, or Stewart maybe, asking me to do ten minutes and I thought it might be fun. I was at a sort of transition time then, so I didn't really try and get more blocks going. I think I only did it two or three times there. I think one of the Polaroids is from there, the one with the fax machine, which I think makes it quite special.

Did the audience love you?

They were more sympathetic than in a straightforward comedy club. They went with the block.

You played the Comedy Store as well, of course.

I had a block kidnapped by someone at the Comedy Store. It was a repetition of my line at the Tunnel Palladium, that "I can go home now," as if that was exactly what I wanted. But the guy who took it was quite aggressive looking, a skinhead. I had all my equipment to protect myself plus my unpredictable persona. I don't know what he

BLOCK #239

BLOCK #243

did with the block. Maybe he took it home and froze it.

And you performed at the Battersea Arts Centre many times.

I did a series of nights, of blocks. It was after my Edinburgh show so I had a little run. I liked that a lot because you get a rhythm.

One of the Battersea blocks somehow came out of the container and then went back into the container from some distance. That was supernatural, I do believe. I'd never had that before. I don't know how it physically happened. It's a mystery. The audience were stunned as well. They thought it was a stunt.

Since we're sitting in Battersea Arts Centre now, I should tell you that I believe in these ghost blocks, which I feel are around, you know what I mean?

Are you saying that you've melted the block but an echo of the block remains?

Yes, it's gone but it's slightly attached to the place, like human ghosts attach to particular houses.

When I sold that painting to Mark Thomas in Bridport, I remembered that I'd melted a block next door at the Bridport Art Centre, so I went up to the door and just sort of sensed it.

I slightly play with the idea, but there's also the idea of what actually happens to these blocks. They melt and evaporate but they still in some way reassemble. Maybe they become rain in the Arctic. I do feel that the blocks have different personalities and I had different relationships with the blocks. You get quite frisky ones that dart all over the place and quite lazy ones too. The combination of being with people and with me changes the block or has some kind of effect on it. If you were doing it alone, the block wouldn't be the same as with an audience. They behave in different ways. Deep! Deep!

BLOCK #368

BLOCK #241

BLOCK #284

BLOCK #171

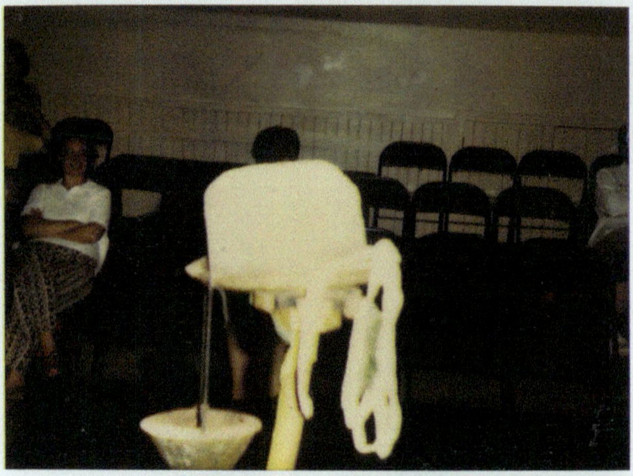

BLOCK #185

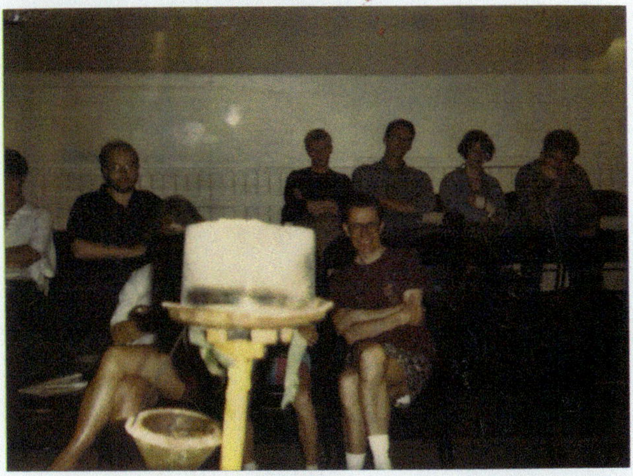

BLOCK #186

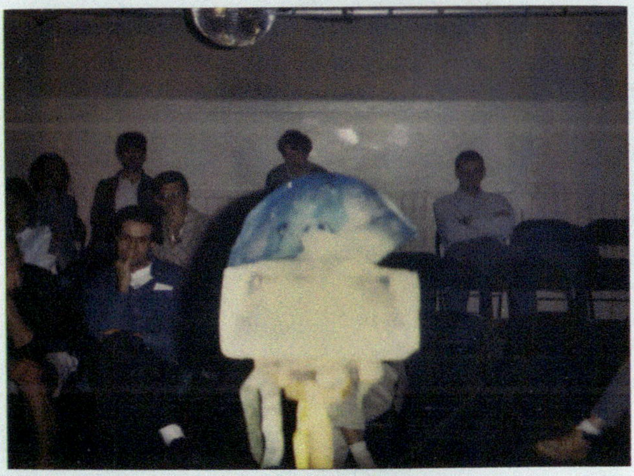

FUNNY BONES (1995)

FUNNY BONES

About your Hollywood moment. Can you tell me what you did for them approximately? Because you're only on the screen for a second.

It's perfectly in keeping with my concept of failure. I didn't know that I'd been cut out. I went along to the premier and I was waiting for my moment and then in the blink of an eye I was gone. I was disappointed but then I thought "how appropriate." I did three days of filming for the director, Peter Chelsom, at Ealing Studios so I thought I was going to have quite a profile from it, but I don't know the reason. I never found out.

How long were you performing for over the three days? Are we talking hours?

Oh, I think probably in total just an hour or so. If that. There was a lot of waiting about. There were lots of people coming and going, Lee Evans and people like that.

And they got it down to a second.

Well, half a second really. [*laughs*]

Maybe they felt it wasn't in keeping with that Music Hall edge. I would say that it was in keeping with it but that's my only theory. I remember one of the assistant people said something along the lines of there not being much to it; I think he'd been expecting some ice sculpture or something. He said it quite rudely in fact. I remembering thinking, "ah, he's got the wrong end of the stick."

I think the crux of the matter may be that the Iceman is really a concept act whereas the other *Funny Bones* acts were probably more skill-based, like George Carl.

It was fascinating seeing [vaudevillian comedian] George Carl and I enjoyed the actual film a lot. I think they did well at getting a lot of researchers and getting people out of the woodwork, including me. Peter Chelsom was very nice but the whole affair was a bit strange. I got to look like a film star without really being in anything.

I remember the casting agents. Fothergill and Lunn, I think they were called. I had to do a block at the audition. I got back in touch with them later and said "would you like me to do some acting?" and they were quite kind really. They wanted me to be in some Jane Austen-type stuff but nothing happened really because I'd left London by that time.

It's a good credit. A nice film to be associated with. Half a second though! You don't want to overexpose yourself, as a cult figure. [*laughs*]

CAKE

BLOCK #259

BLOCK #206

BLOCK #227

BLOCK #619

BLOCK #241

BLOCK #411

AUSTERITY BINGE (2011)

So Stewart Lee got you in to play the Royal Festival Hall?

After my first block, I was promoted to the foyer. This was quite a nice show. Stewart Lee sent [the audience] out from his main show so suddenly I got these batches of people. I quite liked the foyer; it gave me quite a lot of possibilities. It became more about infiltration and I sort of moved about between what had been Stewart's audience and other people who weren't really sure who I was.

Mingling like that is right up Stewart Lee's street, isn't it? He's cited Johnny Vegas as his inspiration for leaving the stage and infiltrating the audience. It completely changes the mood in the room, doesn't it?

Yes! But on that occasion they really didn't know who I was and the block was almost a separate event up on the platform. I only sometimes went up to it.

You were sort of marauding, sort of going about. I was wondering about that photograph of an official-looking woman, maybe a manager, and I wondered if she took issue with what you were doing?

Yes, you can sense that's a bit tense. It was somebody trying to shut me down. I think she relented and we reached a compromise, but it's the sort of thing that did happen. My ice blocks would cause confrontation and then, eventually, peace and harmony.

You seem to be interested in hawking your wares...

Yes, and this show was quite an opportunity. I even remember the names of the people I sold things to, like Kayleigh. And Tobias who actually bought the framed poster of all the blocks.

Did he know about the Iceman already?

I don't know, I don't think so, but he seemed so ecstatic. I can't remember if he knew something about it already or if he just got it right away, but he did treat me like I was a legend. Maybe it's just my charisma.

Does the Iceman's tendency to interact with the audience go back to your time in street theatre?

I always interact with the audience. Like with the breath, or I might go into the audience and blow with them. Or go in and give them a bit of ice. Or the photograph stuff or the fax copies. I like the idea of mingling. It's against some theatrical rules but you break down that fourth wall and it just emphasises the shared experience. At The Hackney Empire [in 2007], I went down into the auditorium and gave them the block and they passed it around. People were amused but they passed it on quite quickly because it was so cold.

Like the Covent Garden block, the RFH foyer block was another durational performance.

Yes, it was quite slow. And it was still quite intact by the end. I pushed it into the River Thames. I did even less to the block than usual. It was a bit of a game. I don't know why. I was more into the idea of selling copies. There are some quite funny photographs of people queuing up. The venue was right on the river so pushing it in was completely spontaneous.

You got people out to watch you dump it in the Thames?

Well, it was more random passersby really. People were saying, "why are you doing that?" It was quite funny. I checked that there was nobody beneath because it was quite a drop.

You might have obliterated someone. It really would have been your last block.

"Iceman kills canoeist." But that's another thing. I don't know what happened to that block. It must have survived for a bit, gone out with the current, maybe returned to Richmond where it came from. It's quite intriguing to think what might have happened to it.

DUCK
WILL
FLOAT
42
Sale
AN

STRAIMING-DOWN NINE

WETNESS IN THE RFH BLUE

A poem by Finn Bush,
ultimate witnice to penultice block

Ecstatic glistening
melting edges with close appreciative people.
One calling "I need Sex." Another: "I'm getting a beer
    don't go —I'm coming back Iceman!"
Another call: "I want to kiss your block!"
And a Canadian teacher shouting about nobody
understanding his important message,
the message of the ice.
Anthony Iceman saying: "I'm in a long term relationship,"
    while counting bullets.
aim pulling his magic act down to the River Thames.
Melt it in the Thaims under street lights.
The riverbank becoming a theatre.
Time and ice suspended, feet on concrete, ice in the air,
    aim's block out over the edge, let go.
Only aim, a clock, one European
    and *H.AIM.S Belfast* seeing the splash.
No malice! Hardice turns out to be the penultimate block
    and not aim's last, drifting in silence
down to Grave's End in the dark.
There's a saint down there.
I, just being a finny fish Iceistant witniced this incoherence.
Aim walks home afterwards acompanied by
    endless urban foxes
Stewart probabLee took a Taxi.

INTO THE THAIMS

BLOCK #1009

BLOCK #203

BLOCK #238

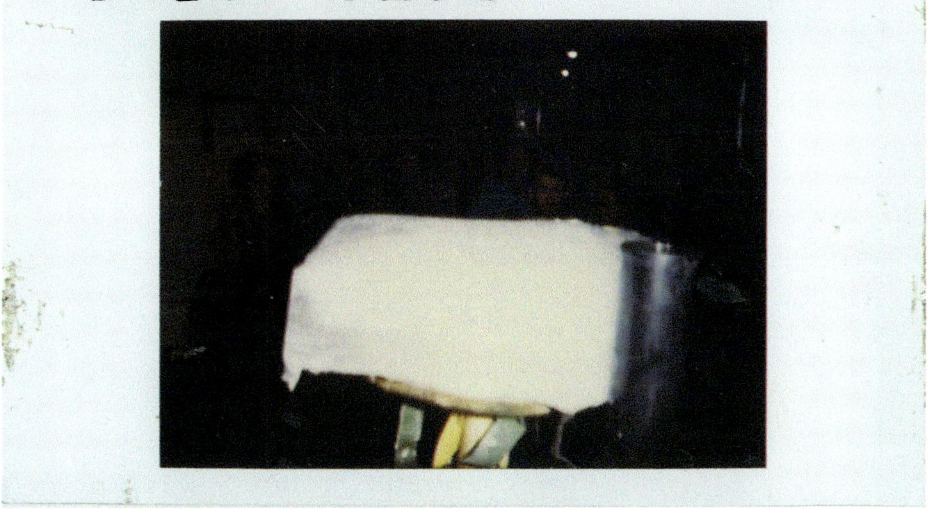

BLOCK #193

PAINTINGS (2014-PRESENT)

CANDLES

How did the ice lead to paintings? What was the process?

It hadn't been a plan and I hadn't painted since I was a kid. But it was all about the blocks living on. I'd got the photographs. I didn't have the confidence that I could paint, and that's confirmed now! But I think it's just an idea. It just came to me that I could paint my blocks, that it would be nice, and I literally went and bought a paint set. I remember feeling quite a lot of trepidation, almost nervousness, and I was always very respectful of the paint and the canvas.

I started doing the photographs but with quite limited paints and they were quite neat compared to some of my later ones. I gradually worked my way through the 56 documented blocks, often capturing their audience, and the duck crops up a lot. Then I painted some 40 or so of the shots from the Royal Festival Hall including one where I drop the block and I look as if I'm dancing with it. Eventually I got bored of interpreting photos so I started to do it more from memory—I even did one of the kangaroo so they're not all ice-based—and now they're largely from imagination. But they're all the same picture in a sense: me and the block. The motif is totally repetitive yet I think there's quite a lot of variety.

It's almost the visual equivalent of the loop.

Yes, and as annoying as the loop. I think some people will be annoyed by it.

But most people will just have one painting on the wall, it's not like they'll have to confront the whole oeuvre.

To be honest, my aim is, because it's so unlikely that I can sell these paintings, to bring myself back to the performance element. It's a challenge. I've only really sold them to people I know so far. I sold one to Mark Thomas when I saw him at his show at the Electric Palace in

Bridport, or rather his partner bought it for him as a present. But I don't know much about the art world and a lot of people don't take my paintings very seriously. Even my friends tend to laugh at it. But I think there's something there and I do like that there's humour to it.

I quite like the mess, which was always a feature of the act, and the accidental effects from the oil and the other elements I use including dirt from the earth.

I really concentrate when I'm painting. I really cut out everything. And I've got my own judgement. I don't let it go until I'm happy with it. I sort of pray a bit before I paint, and I think, and I bless it, and I sometimes take the canvas around for a bit on my head.

Who do you pray to?

That's a bit... private.

Wow!

I pray to what I call The Blockless One. So, I suppose, God really. But I call Him The Blockless One because I feel that the block is my human condition and all the rest of it. Deep!

Basically, I do respect the art and I feel like I'm doing something special with every painting. I don't know if it would be any different if I didn't pray. It has to be.

How do you get along with the more solitary nature of painting compared to your stage work?

I always paint alone. I make a virtue out of excluding anything else that's going on, which annoys my wife. I think even when I used to perform there was a side of me that was quite solitary and it was an effort to overcome the barrier of shyness to get out and interact. So I like the solitariness very much actually. But then again, I do feel I can share it because I can upload the paintings to my *Iceblocked* website plus my Saatchi Art* one and also, eventually, I know that conceivably one will be sold.

*www.saatchiart.com/irvineanthony

BLOCK #281

BLOCK #238

I'm going to stick with the paintings. I might slow down a bit but I'm going to continue with it.

What's your estimation on the number of blocks you've put paid to over the years?

It's probably lower than I'd like it to be. I'm not sure. Under ten thousand.

Do you still melt the occasional block?

No, I don't really perform now. I'm not sure I would even if I were invited.

I think I still use performance in my paintings to an extent. In painting and selling them.

The one at the Royal Festival Hall was almost the last block, the penultimate block really. So I made a virtue of that.

I did a Zoom block in lockdown for the Westminster School Literary Society. And then I've done a couple of radio blocks including one on Radio 4's *Midweek* programme with Libby Purves and Ian Hislop. I feel those are almost live performances even though the audience is down the line.

I did let it go for a number of years but then the documenting idea came back to me and the idea of painting replaced everything. I think that's my main thing now. It's quite a physical effort doing all that stuff, so if I'm not careful I might do a Tommy Cooper and die on stage.

That would be good because you might become famous because of it but also it's failure, which is part of your motif.

Yes! But I might just wait until I'm *really* old.

TOBiAS

BLOCK #192

BLOCK #198

BLOCK #220

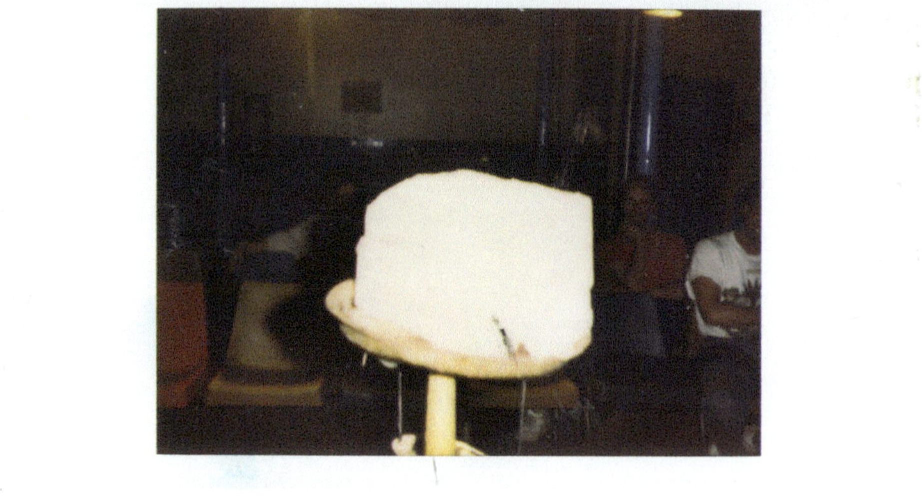

BLOCK #207

BLOCK #312

LEGACY

What do you think of being considered an Outsider Artist? Do you think the term is pejorative and to be resisted or do you think it's true about yourself and to be embraced?

I quite like the label because it makes it sound like I'm a bit "out there." I suppose the performance art is by definition outsiderish because it's not in the middle of things. With the paintings, I quite like the idea of being more of an insider otherwise you get categorised as being slightly on the asylum side of things. I like the idea of being a mainstream painter, which is why I call myself a fine artist.

That's nothing to be ashamed of though. I think it might even be something a lot of people look for in artists and comedians, that they be slightly committable. Spike Milligan for example was a household name.

I was on a TV show with Spike Milligan. It was a Danny Baker special or something. I did a block there. I sensed he was very zany but very clever as well. I remember him saying that all the people in Coventry were deaf from the bombing. Another guy who was there was Hughie Green from *Opportunity Knocks,* and he seemed to rather like the Iceman. He actually suggested a gag. He said I should get special pants that I could put my blowtorch down. I think he thought I was a sort of *Opportunity Knocks* contestant, so he went back in his thinking to that time and gave me advice, which was very sweet really. Danny Baker thought I was going to become very famous.

Do your children enjoy your showbiz anecdotes?

I have one son and I don't think he's very impressed. He's sort of interested but he thinks its maybe a wee bit immature. Our cat, Sabrina, likes to walk over my paintings, especially when wet. My son actually quite likes my paintings but has said I need more variety of themes! My wife thinks the work of aim reflects in part, the Confessional school of poetry.

She likes it then?

Yes, in fact she gave us a blurb for the book. "aim's Absurdist Confessional work celebrates the poignant and the joyous. But he's always very possessive of the fridge."—Mrs. Iceman.

That's perfect. With regards to the book...

I do like the idea of the blocks living on. And I do like how it's quite arbitrary and accidental what does and doesn't survive.

One copy of this book will go to the British Library and be on the shelf forever.

Yes, I like that, I think that's good.

Well, is that good? I was going to ask if the book defeats the object of your act, if what we're doing will immortalise what should have been transient. You used the medium of transience.

No, I like the idea of that a lot because the idea is, in spite of the transience and the actual disappearance, the transformation of the block, they survive. I'm very keen on the idea that *in* the perishable blocks there's something about as imperishable as you can get, getting it into the British Library.

The National Librarians will defend it with their lives.

When the world finally implodes, it could be the last thing that goes.

People do remember you.

Modest as I am, I do forget that people know who I am. The *C86* podcast with David Eastaugh came out of the blue. He just emailed me through my website, a very minimal type of message, "I would like to interview you," and then we just fixed a date and we did it. I actually had a block there because even though it's radio I

CONTEMPLATION

BLOCK #283

like the idea of nobody being able to see it but doing it anyway.

I think he's getting annoyed with me because I emailed him the painting [of the block] and his emails are getting even more minimal now. Actually, he was very pleased to get a Polaroid of the block.

I believe in a blockless future.

What do you mean?

That's my final comment.

Can I interpret it?

Well, the blocks will stop for me anyway. I think that's what I'm getting at. My mortality.

But people will still make and melt blocks after you're gone. Your friends at Eskimo Ice for example.

Ice will go on but not in the same format. But our book will be selling out at that point! Thousands of copies!

BLOCK #171

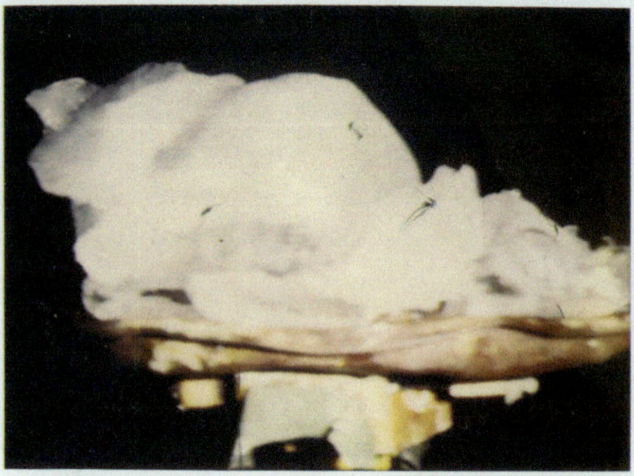

BLOCK #188

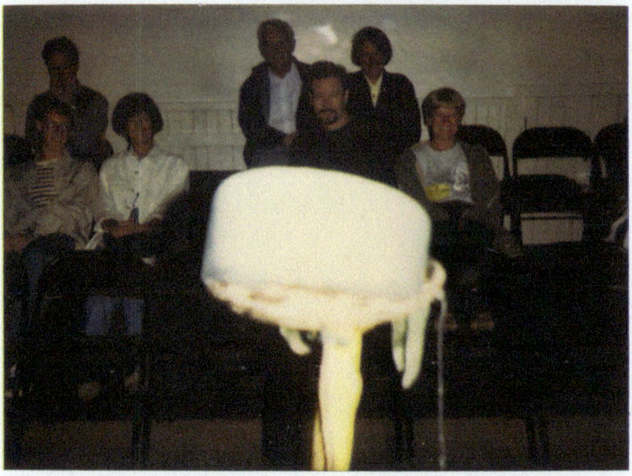

BLOCK #194

BLOCK #237

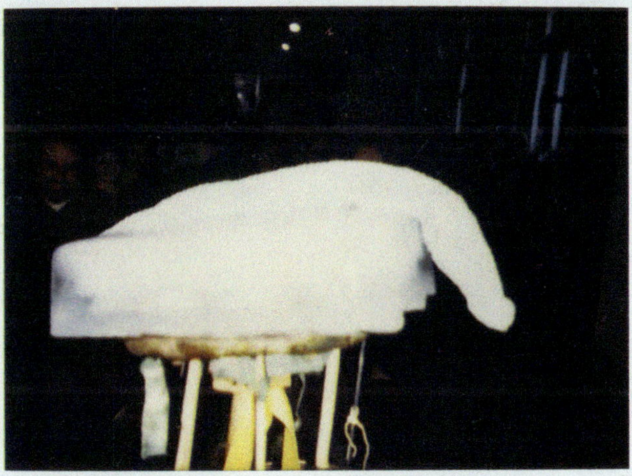

FOYER

BLOCKS REMEMBERED

The ledger containing every numbered block is long lost, but we found the locations of a few melts.

BLOCK 1:
Melted
at Crazy Larry's, Chelsea

BLOCK 69:
Melted
at Banana Cabaret, Balham

BLOCK 125:
Melted
at the Rub-a-Dub club,
Sydenham

BLOCK 212-215:
Melted
at the Calton Centre,
Edinburgh

BLOCK 228:
Melted
at Ealing Studios
for *Funny Bones* film

BLOCK 259:
Given to a journalist
"as a bribe"

BLOCKS 260-276:
Melted
at the Pleasance Theatre,
Edinburgh

BLOCK 281:
Melted
at Battersea Arts Centre

BLOCK 282:
Melted
at Battersea Arts Centre

BLOCK 283:
Melted
[at unknown nightclub]
in Glasgow

BLOCK 284:
Melted
at Theatre Royal,
Drury Lane

BLOCK 297:
Melted
at Bath Comedy Festival

STEW

AFTERWORD

I am so glad this book exists. The Iceman has been an inspiration to me since I first saw him, melting his ice, downstairs at The King's Head in Crouch End in 1989. I don't really know why I loved his act so much. I didn't really like the puns, which I thought spoiled it a bit, but I loved the idea of trying to formalise the process of turning ice into water, something which would happen anyway if the ice was simply left to its own devices.

The Iceman's turn was one of those acts that left some people in hysterics and others furious. Sometimes it became funny again to an extreme degree, after it had seemed to have died. Other times people giggled and burbled all the way through. But the Iceman's act never actually failed. As long as some of the ice became water, which it always did, it had at least partially succeeded on its own terms. I think his influence on my stand-up is fairly obvious, now I come to describe what I liked about him.

I met the Iceman out in the real world only once. In 1995 I woke up on a Sunday morning on the floor of someone I didn't know after ending up at a party in a North London suburb. At 6 am I slipped out into the anonymous streets and wandered about—this was pre-satnav and mobile phone—trying to work out where I was. Suddenly I saw the Iceman, distant in the sunny morning haze, loading an ice block wrapped in hessian into his van, parked between London Planes and rusting cars. "Do you live here?", I asked. He said he didn't, but told me had fridges in the hallways of shared houses all around the country where he had ice blocks ready for him to pick up, as he couldn't be sure of making a long journey and keeping the ice intact, not owning a refrigerated vehicle. But writing this now I wonder, did I imagine it?

I carried on seeing the Iceman's shows—somewhere I have a fax and a Polaroid from his mid-'90s Edinburgh show—and yes, he did guest in Simon's Cluub Zarathustra cabaret. When I had my own Sunday morning chat show on Resonance 104.4 FM in the early noughties I invited him on to melt his ice live on air in central London, which was amusing to me, as it was probably the worst radio idea ever. People would be at home listening to ice melt.

The studio was the traditional broom cupboard size. The other guest was the cantankerous comedy poet John Dowie. The Iceman tried to melt the ice with antifreeze, which was dangerous in a confined space, and people began choking and rubbing their eyes and running out. Dowie was quite angry about it, I remember. I helped the Iceman carry the remaining ice to his car, which didn't look roadworthy, and neither did he. I worried about him, to be honest.

The last time I saw the Iceman was at The Royal Festival Hall show. I booked him but we didn't meet. I was busy running the stage show in the big room, but at one point I went out into the foyer and saw the Iceman on a balcony looking down at me. We waved at each other. And that was that.

I love the Iceman. He is a blank canvas. You project your own ideals onto him: fun, single-mindedness, commitment, a love of life and its inherent absurdity. I am fascinated to learn a little of his origins in this book, another of Wringham's essential mini-masterpieces, but I am relieved that it leaves me as baffled and delighted as I was the first time I saw the ice block fail to melt. The world is increasingly stripped of wonder and mystery. The Iceman carries within him an essence of the unknowable, of the not quite thereness that makes life worth living. Whatever next?

STEWART LEE, WRITER-CLOWN
STOKE NEWINGTON
HALLOWEEN 2022

ACKNOWLEDGEMENTS

We'd both like to thank John Fleming, Simon Munnery, Stewart Lee, Battersea Arts Centre, the Alan Dimmick Photographic Archive, Chris Evans, and Finn Bush.

Rob would like to thank Samara Leibner, Ian Macpherson, Timothy and Rowan Eyre, Andy Holden, Gabriel Featherstone, Ian Shuttleworth, and Oliver Double.

Anthony would like to thank his freezer.

Also Available from Go Faster Stripe

How To Live

by Simon Munnery

"One of the funniest, most original comedians of the past 20 years" — *The Guardian*

If you don't read this book you ought to be ashamed of yourself.

If you do, you will be.

Simon Munnery's manual for a better life is now back in print.

It's small and short, like life. Each page has a crafty, witty one liner on it. You can whizz through all of them in 5 minutes, or maybe mull them over at a rate of one per day.

This special GFS edition is an almost exact facsimile of the the original Pictures on Walls design.

Also Available from Go Faster Stripe

Stern Plastic Owl

by Robert Wringham

"Delightful and insightful and quite simply rightful, Robert Wringham's observations and commentaries on our strange old world make everything better." — Ben Moor

Meet Robert Wringham. He strides across the landscape of a slightly fantastical world. It's the same world that you and I live in... only more so.

It's a STERN world.

It's a PLASTIC world.

You'd better believe it's an OWL world.

It's the world of the STERN PLASTIC I-KNOW-NOT-WHAT.

Is it possible to walk through a duckpond using a corncob pipe for air? Just what was H.G. Wells like in bed? And how high can you raise the eyebrow before it interferes with the flightpaths of planes?

Deft Mr. Wringham skirts around these questions and more in his latest collection of what the *Financial Times* recently described as "some dope shit"*, some thirty classic pieces tenderly gouged from their original contexts and artfully mashed into book form.

**they said no such thing.*

www.gofasterstripe.com